C000104242

The Rationale Of Mesmerism

C. W. Leadbeater

Kessinger Publishing's Rare Reprints

Thousands of Scarce and Hard-to-Find Books on These and other Subjects!

- Americana
- Ancient Mysteries
- Animals
- Anthropology
- Architecture
- Arts
- Astrology
- Bibliographies
- Biographies & Memoirs
- Body, Mind & Spirit
- Business & Investing
- Children & Young Adult
- Collectibles
- Comparative Religions
- Crafts & Hobbies
- Earth Sciences
- Education
- Ephemera
- Fiction
- Folklore
- Geography
- Health & Diet
- History
- Hobbies & Leisure
- Humor
- Illustrated Books
- Language & Culture
- Law
- Life Sciences
- Literature
- Medicine & Pharmacy
- Metaphysical
- Music
- Mystery & Crime
- Mythology
- Natural History
- Outdoor & Nature
- Philosophy
- Poetry
- Political Science
- Science
- Psychiatry & Psychology
- Reference
- Religion & Spiritualism
- Rhetoric
- Sacred Books
- Science Fiction
- Science & Technology
- Self-Help
- Social Sciences
- Symbolism
- Theatre & Drama
- Theology
- Travel & Explorations
- War & Military
- Women
- Yoga
- *Plus Much More!*

We kindly invite you to view our catalog list at:
http://www.kessinger.net

THIS ARTICLE WAS EXTRACTED FROM THE BOOK:

Some Glimpses of Occultism

BY THIS AUTHOR:

C. W. Leadbeater

ISBN 0766146960

READ MORE ABOUT THE BOOK AT OUR WEB SITE:

http://www.kessinger.net

KESSINGER
PUBLISHING

OR ORDER THE COMPLETE
BOOK FROM YOUR FAVORITE STORE

ISBN 0766146960

Because this article has been extracted from a parent book, it may have non-pertinent text at the beginning or end of it.

Any blank pages following the article are necessary for our book production requirements. The article herein is complete.

CHAPTER VI.

THE RATIONALE OF MESMERISM.

This subject of mesmerism must be, I think, one of considerable interest to every one who understands at all what it includes. There is a great deal of misconception as to the signification of the word, so it is well to commence with some sort of definition. In these days we hear little of mesmerism, but much of hypnotism, and the question at once arises, are these two things the same? I believe myself that we may usefully make a distinction between them, though many people use them practically as synonyms. Hypnotism is derived from the Greek word *hupnos,* sleep; so that hypnotism is the study of the art of putting to sleep. The word, however, has rather unfortunate associations, and a history behind it which is far from creditable. There is no question that originally the name of mesmerism was applied to all phenomena which are now covered by the other, because Mesmer was, as far as Europe is concerned, the discoverer of the power which has been called after him. He was ridiculed and persecuted by the ignorant and prejudiced scientific men of his time, and the medical profession would have nothing to say to his experiments. They simply denied the facts, just as many people now think it intelligent to deny facts of spiritualism.

Fifty years later a certain Mr. Braid, a surgeon of Manchester, published a little book approaching these facts from a new standpoint, and stated that they were all due to the fatigue of certain muscles of the eyelid. He called his book *Neurypnology,* and there are still many who suppose him to be the first man to treat these subjects scientifically. This, however, by no means represents the facts, for his hypothesis leaves most of the phenomena unaccounted for; and it seems to have won official acceptance only because it offered a line of retreat from an untenable position. The phenomena which the profession had decided to ridicule and deny were constantly recurring; here was a method by which they could at least partially be admitted without having to make the humiliating confession that Mesmer had after all been right, and orthodox science wrong. So the theory was set up that this was in reality an entirely new discovery, and must be called by a distinct name. Along this line followed Charcot, Binet and Feré, and a number of recent writers—all taking but a partial view of the subject, all ignoring any facts which did not square with this partial view.

Mesmer himself, the real pioneer of this line of discovery, came much nearer to the facts in the opinions which he expressed. He held the existence of a subtle fluid which passes from the operator to the subject, and in this correct assumption he was followed by the earlier French experimenters, the Marquis de Puységur, Deleuze, Baron de Potet and Baron von Reichenbach.

The Experiments of Reichenbach.

The last-named patiently tried and recorded a long series of experiments with sensitives, and his works deserve careful study. His first discovery was that certain young people among his patients could, in a dark room, see flames issuing from the poles of a magnet; then a little later he found that similar flames were seen flowing from the tips of his fingers while he was engaged in making mesmeric passes. It was because of this similarity that he bestowed upon the fluid which is transferred from the operator to the patient in mesmerism the name of "animal magnetism." He suspected its connection with the vital force poured forth from the sun, and confirmed his idea by an ingenious experiment. He arranged a copper wire so that one end should be exposed to the sunlight out of doors, and the other he led into his dark room. He then found that if the outer end of the wire was kept in the shade, the sensitive in the room saw nothing; but if the wire was exposed to the sunlight, the patient was at once able to point out the end of the wire in the dark room, because a faint light began to issue from it. When a copper plate was attached to the outer end of the wire, so as to collect more of the sun's power, quite a brilliant light was discernable by the sensitive.

Through all his earlier experiments he was under the impression that this magnetic sensitiveness was always a symptom of ill-health, and it seems to have been a great surprise to him when he found that one of his patients retained her power after her recovery. Further investigation led him to understand that its possession was not a question of health but of psychic faculty; and he conjectures, correctly enough, that all in reality have the power to a greater or less degree, but that in some it is only able to come to the surface when the ordinary physical faculties are weakened by sickness. It will at once be seen that these earlier writers were much nearer to the truth about such matters than many of their successors have been.

Even at the present day there are probably no better records of cases of surgical operations under mesmerism, and of curative mesmerism generally, than those contained in the books of Dr. Esdaile of Calcutta, and of Dr. Elliotson, who was working in North London. At about that period—in 1842, I think it was—considerable attention was attracted by an operation performed at St. Bartholomew's Hospital in London by a Mr. Ward, who amputated above the knee the leg of a patient who had been put into the mesmeric trance—as good a case as the most sceptic enquirer could desire. Yet when a report of this case was laid before the Royal Medical and

Chirurgical Society of London, they declined to listen to
the testimony, on the ground that it was manifestly in-
credible and absurd, and that even if it were true it would
be contrary to the will of Providence, since pain was in-
tended to be part of a surgical operation! It seems impossible that any assemblage of educated and presumably
scientific men could be so idiotic, but there is no doubt
that this resolution was passed and still stands on record.

Invincible Ignorance.

Things have improved since then, but there is still a
good deal of foolish incredulity with regard to this subject—and, worse still, a great deal of unfounded assertion
on the part of the ignorant, to which it is difficult for the
student to listen with patience. On this point Mr. Sinnett, our Vice-President, has well written:—"No one de-
serves blame for leaving altogether unstudied any subject that does not attract him. But in most cases people
who are conscious of limited intellectual resources enter-
tain a decent respect for others who are better furnished.
A man may be nothing but a sportsman himself, and yet
refrain from asserting that chemists and electricians must
be imposters, and a chemist may know nothing of Italian
art, and yet may refrain from declaring that Raphael
never existed. But all through the commonplace world
people who are ignorant of psychic science encourage
one another in the brainless and absurd denial of facts,
whenever any of its phenomena come up for treatment.
The average country grocer, the average reporter, the
average student of physical science, are all steeped in
the same dense incapacity to understand the propriety of
respecting the knowledge of others, even if they do not
share it themselves, whenever they brush up against any
statement relating to the work of those who are engaged
in any branch of psychic enquiry. From the occult point
of view, indeed, one can understand why this should be

so, for the incredulity of unspiritual mankind is Nature's own protection against those unfit as yet to use her higher spiritual gifts."

The book from which that quotation is made is called *The Rationale of Mesmerism,* and it is one which no student of this subject should neglect to read, for it puts the Theosophical theory of the matter much more ably than I can, the author being a practical mesmerist of considerable power and experience. All that I can do is to give you an outline sketch; for the filling in I must refer you to Mr. Sinnett. It is impossible to understand mesmerism unless we take it as part of an orderly scheme of the universe, and explain it in accordance with the facts which are known about the constitution of man, and his relation to the world around him. Taken in that way, it at once becomes comprehensible, and no difficulty is found in classifying and accounting for its various manifestations. We must remember the Theosophical explanation of the different planes of nature and the corresponding bodies possessed by man; for since the fluid poured out in mesmerism is subtle and invisible to ordinary sight, it will obviously affect the subtler part of the body, and consequently it is to our study of that part that we must turn for a rational theory of its effects. It is well always to remember that man is a being living simultaneously in two worlds—the seen and the unseen; existing simultaneously upon several of these planes of nature, and consciously or unconsciously receiving impressions from them all through his life.

When we realize this we are prepared to understand how partial any merely physical view of man must be, and how easily we may miscalculate actions and happenings on this plane, if we are ignorant of their causes on higher levels. Mr. Sinnett, in the book just mentioned, compares our position in that respect to that of a fish which, swimming in the water, tries to understand the motions of the keel of a ship as it moves beside him. He will no doubt be able to comprehend the resistance offered by the water to the keel, its deflection from a straight course by currents, and so on; but there must frequently appear motions of the reason of which he can have no conception, because it belongs to another and higher world. The slope given to the hull of the vessel by the setting of the sails this way or that would be to him a mysterious and unaccountable movement, and he would probably suppose it to be due to a living will residing in the creature. A flying fish might conceivably learn to understand something of the conditions both of the air and the sea, and so would come nearer to a correct theory; and in this respect the clairvoyant student is like the flying fish—he is able to transcend his element to some extent, and so to enter a wider world, in which he learns many lessons. The thoughts and passions of the man are seen on the physical plane only by their effects, yet they are the motive power, and must be taken into account if we wish to understand, just as our suppositions fish would have to know something about sails before he could know why his ship moved as it did.

We may approach this subject of mesmerism along one of two lines. We may either commence to make practical experiments for ourselves, or we may take up the study of experiments of others through the books which have been written. To any man who decides for the books, I should recommend Dr. Esdaile's as the best of all to begin with; for his subjects were all Orientals, and they are on the average far more sensitive to mesmeric influence than white men are.

The Nature of Sensitiveness.

That does not mean that they are necessarily of weaker will; it is a question of the side of the man which is developed. You may remember how I have explained in previous lectures that the evolution of man is cyclical in its character—that it consists in a descent into matter and then a rising out of it again, bearing the results of the immersion in experience gained and quality developed. There comes in the course of this cycle a lowest point, at which the man is most deeply buried in matter, and consequently least open to any influences from subtler forces, and this point of extreme materiality is often coincident with strong intellectual development. In this way we have a combination of a grossly material nature with a specially materialistic mental attitude; and just at that period the man would certainly not be a good subject mesmerically. I do not say that his resistance might not be overcome by a sufficiently strong will, but it would require more effort than it would be in the least likely to be worth while to make, and so we should call him a bad subject.

Before that there would be a period when the psychic side of him could be much more readily reached, and again later in his evolution it would reappear, though at this second stage it would hardly be possible to control him mesmerically except with his own consent, for this is the truer psychism in which the man possesses his powers in full consciousness, and can use them voluntarily efficiently. But at the intermediate point it is not the amount of intellect which he possesses which saves him from mesmeric influence, as he often proudly thinks, but simply the materialism of his conceptions. It is because he is tied down to the merely physical plane that he resists any effort to impress him in that way from without.

When, however, an impression can be made, the effects are often of the most striking character. Not only may one person subjugate the will of another to almost any conceivable extent, but physical results may be produced such as anaesthesia or rigidity, and many diseases may be readily cured. How is all this to be explained? We must remember that the physical body contains a great deal of matter that is invisible to ordinary sight. Not only has it its solid and liquid constituents, but there is also much that is gaseous, and a great deal that is etheric. This latter constituent plays no small part in the man's well-being, for the whole of his body is permeated by it, so that if it were possible to withdraw from him all the solid, liquid and gaseous particles, the form of his body would still be clearly marked out in etheric matter. This part of his body, which has sometimes been called the etheric double, is the vehicle of vitality in the man.

The Nervous Circulation.

We know that besides the system of veins and arteries, we have a system of nerves running all through the body; and just as arteries and veins have circulation, whose centre is the heart, so have the nerves their cirlation, whose centre is the brain. But it is a circulation not of blood but of the life-fluid, and it flows not so much along the nerves themselves as along a sort of coating of ether which surrounds each nerve. Many electricians have thought it probable that electricity does not flow along a wire at all, but along a coating of ether surrounding the wire; and if that be so, the phenomenon is exactly duplicated by this flowing of the vital force.

Normally in the healthy man two types of fluid are connected with this system of nervous circulation. First, there is the nerve-aura, which flows regularly and steadily round from the brain as a centre; and secondly, there is this vital fluid, which is absorbed from without and carried round by the nerve-aura in the form of rose-coloured particles, which are easily visible to clairvoyant sight. Let us consider the nerve-aura first. It has been observed that upon the presence of this fluid depends the proper working of the nerve—a fact which can be demonstrated by various experiments. We know that it is possible by mesmeric passes to make a person's arm quite insensible to pain; this is done by driving back this nerve-aura, so that over that part of the body the flow is no longer kept up, and consequently the nerve is unable to report to the brain what touches it, as it usually does. Without the specialized ether which normally surrounds it, the nerve is not able to communicate with the brain, and so it is precisely as though the nerve were not there for the time—or in other words, there is no feeling.

The vital fluid is also specialized, and in the healthy man it is present in great abundance. It is poured upon us originally from the sun, which is the source of life in this inner sense as well as, by means of its light and heat, in the outer world. The atoms in the earth's atmosphere are more or less charged with this force at all times, though it is in much greater activity and abundance in brilliant sunshine; and it is only by absorbing it that our physical bodies are able to live. In itself it is naturally invisible, like all other forces; but we see its effect in the intense activity of the atoms energized by it. After it has been absorbed into the human body and thereby specialized, these atoms take on the beautiful rose-colour already described, and are carried in a constant stream over and through the whole body along the nerves. The man in perfect health has plenty of this fluid to spare, and it is constantly radiating from his body in all directions, so that he is in truth shedding strength and vitality on those around him, even though quite unconsciously. On the other hand, a man who from weakness or other causes is unable to specialize for his own use a sufficient amount of the world's life-force, sometimes equally unconsciously acts as a sponge, and absorbs the already specialized vitality of any sensitive person with whom he comes in contact, to his own temporary benefit, no doubt, but often to the serious injury of his victim. Probably most persons have experienced this in a minor degree, and have found that there is some one among their acquaintances after whose visits they always feel an unaccountable weakness and languor.

What the Mesmerist Gives.

Now you will begin to see what it is that the mesmerizer pours into his subject. It may be either the nerve-ether or the vitality, or both. Supposing a patient to be seriously weakened or exhausted, so that he has lost power to specialize the life-fluid for himself, the mesmerizer may renew his stock by pouring some of his own upon the quivering nerves, and so produce a rapid recovery. The process is analogous to what is often done in the case of food. When a person reaches a certain stage of weakness the stomach loses the power to digest, and so the body is not properly nourished, and the weakness is thereby increased. The remedy adopted in that case is to present to the stomach food already partially digested by means of pepsin or other similar preparations; this can probably be assimilated, and thus strength is gained. Just so, a man who is unable to specialize for himself may still absorb what has already been specialized by another, and so gains strength to make an effort to resume the normal action of the etheric organs. In many cases of weakness that is all that is needed.

There are other instances in which congestion of some kind has taken place, the vital fluid has not circulated properly, and the nerve-aura is sluggish and unhealthy. Then the obvious course of proceeding is to replace it by healthy nerve-ether from without; but there are several ways in which this may be done. Some magnetizers simply employ brute force, and steadily pour in resistless floods of their own ether in the hope of washing away that which needs removal. Success may be attained along these lines, though with the expenditure of a good deal more energy than is necessary. A more scientific method is that which goes to work somewhat more quietly, and first withdraws the congested or diseased matter, and then replaces it by healthier nerve-ether thus gradually stimulating the sluggish current into activity. If the man has a headache, for example, there will almost certainly be a congestion of unhealthy ether about some part of his brain, and the first step is to draw that away.

How is this to be managed? Just in the same way as the outpouring of strength is managed—by an exercise of the will. We must not forget that these finer subdivisions of matter are readily moulded or affected by the action of the human will. The mesmerist may make passes, but they are at most nothing but the pointing of his gun in a certain direction, while his will is the powder that moves the ball and produces the result, the fluid being the shot sent out. A mesmerizer who understands his business can manage as well without passes if he wishes; I have known one who never employed them, but simply looked at his subject. The only use of the hand is to concentrate the fluid, and perhaps to help the imagination of the operator; for to will strongly he must believe, and the action no doubt makes it easier for him to realize what he is doing. Just as a man may pour out magnetism by an effort of will, so may he draw it away by an effort of will, though in this case also he may often use a gesture of the hands to help him. In dealing with the headache, he would probably lay his hands upon the forehead of the patient, and think of them as sponges steadily drawing out the unhealthy magnetism from the brain. That he is actually producing the result of which he thinks, he will probably soon discover; for unless he takes precautions to cast off the bad magnetism which he is absorbing, he will either himself feel the headache or begin to suffer from a pain in the arm and hand with which the operation is being performed. He is actually drawing into himself diseased matter, and it is necessary for his comfort and well-being that he should dispose of it before it obtains a permanent lodgment in his body.

He should therefore adopt some definite plan to get rid of it, and the simplest is just to throw it away, to shake it from the hands as one would shake water. Although he does not see it, the matter which he has withdrawn is physical, and can be dealt with by physical means. It is therefore necessary that he should not neglect these precautions, and that he should not forget to wash his hands carefully after curing a headache or any malady of that nature. Then, after he has removed the cause of the evil, he proceeds to pour in good strong healthy magnetism to take its place, and to protect the patient against the return of the disease. One can see that in the case of any nervous affection this method would have manifold advantages. In most of such cases what is wrong is an irregularity of the fluids which course along the nerves; either they are congested, or they are sluggish in their flow, or on the other hand they may be too rapid; they may be deficient in quantity, or poor in quality. Now if we administer drugs of any sort, at the best we can only act upon the physical nerve, and through it to some limited extent upon the fluids surrounding it; whereas mesmerism acts directly upon the fluids themselves, and so goes straight to the root of the evil.

Magnetic Sympathy.

In those other cases where trance is produced, or where the rigidity of the muscles is one of the results, the will of the operator is also concerned, and force of some sort is always poured in. But the will is somewhat differently directed; instead of thinking of curing, or of withdrawing evil magnetism, the mesmerizer is thinking of dominating the will of the subject, or of replacing the man's nerve-aura either partially or entirely by his own. When this latter is the case, the subject's nerves no longer report to his brain, but a close sympathy is created between the two persons concerned. This may be made to work in two ways—so that the operator feels instead of the subject, or that the subject feels everything that touches the operator. I have seen instances in which, while the subject was entranced, the operator stood with his hands behind him a few yards away; and if some third person pricked the hand of the operator (hidden behind his back, so that the sensitive could by no possibility see it in the ordinary way) the subject would immediately rub the corresponding hand, as though she had felt the prick instead of the mesmerizer. Presumably his nerve-ether was in connection with her brain instead of her own, and when she received from this aura the feeling that she would have otherwise associated with a prick in her hand, she supposed it to come from its usual source, and acted accordingly.

This is after all only a phenomenon of precisely the same nature as that which we observe when a man has had his arm removed by an operation; sometimes something will cause irritation to one of the nerves which were originally connected with the fingers, and his brain will refer this sensation to its accustomed cause, and the man will assert that he feels pain in the amputated limb. Another analogous experiment is made in optical study; it is possible to produce a slight electrical discharge inside a person's head, thus affecting the optic nerve at an intermediate point, instead of through the retina of the eye. When this is done, the brain registers the flash as though it had come through the ordinary channel, and it seems to the man that he has seen a flash external to himself. The brain instinctively refers the impression which it receives to the source from which such impressions have always hitherto come. It is as though we should tap a telegraph wire at an intermediate point, and send a message thence; the operator at each end would suppose that the message came from the operator at the other; it would not occur to them that the signals which had always hitherto come from the other station were now caused at an intermediate point.

The Phenomena.

We now begin to glimpse the method in which mesmeric phenomena are produced. This nerve-aura or nerve-ether is the intermediary on the one hand between will and physical action, and on the other between the impressions received upon the physical plane and the mind which accepts and analyzes them. So when the mesmerist substitutes his own nerve-aura for that of the subject he can control both the actions and sensations of his patient. The nerves which normally bear messages from the man's own brain now bring them from a different brain; but the muscles, receiving their message through the accustomed channel, obey it unhesitatingly, and so the man can be made to do all kinds of foolish and incongruous actions. On the other hand, since the reception and translation of all impressions from without depends upon this nerve-aura, when it is under foreign control any illusion may be conveyed to the undeveloped and therefore undiscerning ego.

I remember seeing a good instance of that in Burma. Our president-founder, Colonel H. S. Olcott, is a good mesmerist, and I have seen him try many interesting experiments. I recollect that in one case he threw into the mesmeric condition a native servant who could not speak English. The man seemed as usual, and was not in any obvious kind of trance, yet as to impressions he was absolutely under the control of the Colonel's will. Our president asked (in English) what illusion should be produced, and some one suggested that a line of fire should be seen in a certain part of the room. The Colonel made one strong pass in the direction indicated, thereby creating a vigorous thought-form; and then the servant was called up and told to walk around the room. He moved quite naturally until he reached the imaginary line, when he manifested symptoms of great surprise and terror and cried out that there was fire in the way, and that he could not pass. In another case the Colonel drew an imaginary line on the ground and willed that the servant should be unable to pass over it—the man of course not being present. The servant was then called by his master, and came briskly as usual; but when he reached the imaginary line he stumbled and almost fell, and as he recovered himself he declared that he must be bewitched, since something held his feet, so that he could not move. And though he made several efforts, he was evidently unable to cross that imaginary line, though he was much puzzled and frightened to find himself in such an incomprehensible dilemma.

I have seen many such instances as that, and I think they at once show us how dangerous this power might become in the hands of an unscrupulous man. This servant appeared normal, and no one could have supposed him to be in any unusual condition, yet he was entirely under delusion; therefore he could easily have been led into foolish or even criminal action under the influence of some other imposed delusion. Experiments have shown that in such cases action may be delayed—that a person may be impressed to do a certain thing, say, at three o'clock tomorrow, and then awakened from the mesmeric influence. But at three o'clock tomorrow a sudden uncontrollable impulse will come over him to do that thing, and in the vast majority of cases he will at once proceed to do it. Uncontrollable is perhaps too strong a word for it, for no impulse is really that; but this thought which will arise within the man is in no way distinguishable from a thought or impulse of his own, and most men do not greatly reason about their impulses, or make much effort to weigh and govern them. If the act ordered were an immoral one, a good and pure subject would be much horrified, and a struggle would arise, which might end in submission to the impulse or victory over it. I am sorry to say that some unscrupulous experiments of that sort have been tried in Paris—experiments which I should consider immoral and unjustifiable. Their results have shown that there are cases in which innate virtue is strong enough to triumph over even the most determined attempt to compel it to violate its conscience; but in the majority of instances the temptation prevailed. You see therefore how necessary it is that every mesmerist should be good and pure-hearted, as he might readily be tempted to misuse so terrible a power.

A Word of Caution.

For this reason among others it is not well to dabble in mesmerism or to play with it. All psychic forces are distinctly edged tools for the inexperienced person, and all who take up the investigation of any of them will do well to prepare themselves by an exhaustive study of the results attained by their predecessors, for it is only when armed with knowledge and shielded by purity of intention and selflessness that the neophyte can be certain of safety. All these things—mesmerism, spiritualism, telepathy, *et id genus omne*—should be taken up seriously and scientifically if they are taken up at all. As Mr. Stead remarks with regard to similar studies: "If you cannot or will not examine the subject seriously, you had a thousand times better leave it alone. It is unwise for a boy to go fooling round a buzz-saw. Anybody with a smattering of chemistry can manufacture dynamite, but the promiscuous experimenting with high explosives is more likely to result in explosion than profit. And if you feel disposed to go in 'for the fun of the thing,' every serious investigator has only one word to say, and that is—*don't!*"

There is no need, however, for the peaceable member of the peaceable public to go about in fear of having gruesome and uncanny currents of mesmeric influence poured upon him from unexpected directions. It is quite easy for any ordinary person to resist any effort on the part of another to act upon him in this way, and in all the terrible cases of which we hear, where some weak-willed victim is used as a tool in the hands of an unscrupulous villain, we may be sure that there has been a long series of previous experiments, to which the victim willingly lent himself, before that baneful control was so firmly established. It is only in novels that one glance from the eye of the bold, bad man reduces the unfortunate heroine to abject submission. In real life those who are unselfish and determined need have no fear.

In close connection with mesmerism is the study of the various types of clairvoyance which may be developed under its influence; but I have devoted several lectures recently to clairvoyance, so I am purposely omitting special reference to that subject now. The connection is simply that before the higher faculties can be employed the lower must be controlled, and as many persons have not yet learnt to do this for themselves, it is only when some external repression is applied that their inner senses have any opportunity of action. But in all cases it is better for the man to manage his own affairs, and wait for psychic powers until he can obtain them naturally in the course of his evolution, without needing the application of force from without to aid him in conquering his own lower nature. Steady natural development is always the safest and best; and the character is in all cases the first point to which training should be applied.

Let him educate his heart, that it shall be pure and true; and his intellect, that he may be balanced by common-sense and reason; so shall he be ready for psychic faculty and mesmeric power when they come to him, and as of old, it still remains true "Seek ye first the kingdom of God and His righteousness, and all these things shall be added unto you."

This is the end of this publication.

Any remaining blank pages are for our book binding
requirements and are blank on purpose.

To search thousands of interesting publications like this one,
please remember to visit our website at:

http://www.kessinger.net

CPSIA information can be obtained at www.ICGtesting.com
Printed in the USA
BVOW07s0956260314

348846BV00007B/132/P

9 781162 844893